THE LIFE OF TEXAS JACK:

EIGHT YEARS A CRIMINAL,

41 YEARS TRUSTING GOD.

By

Nathaniel Reed

D1472234

Contents

Preface

I have spent numerous hours and miles collecting the information in the book. I have tried to make this as true to the original text as possible only correcting obvious name spellings and typos that interfered with the text. The story is one of an outlaw and lawman both raised up together in the wilds of Arkansas.

I hope my efforts will help preserve this history of Madison County, Arkansas

I dedicate this book to my wife Jackie who supports me in any project

Scott Hensley

THE LIFE OF TEXAS JACK: EIGHT YEARS A CRIMINAL, 41 YEARS TRUSTING GOD.

Chapter I

MY EARLY LIFE.

Nathaniel Reed is my name, and my native state is Arkansas. I was born March 23, 1862. My father was a Union soldier, and died November 16, 1863. My mother was left a widow with two sons to support. Later she married a man who was kind to me until her death which occurred October 14, 1875. Within three months my step-father married a dutch widow with thirteen children and trouble begin for me. I was treated with great cruelty, but battled as hard with hardship as a lad of thirteen could with strangers. I was timid and chicken hearted and everything seemed to go wrong with me.

At last I could endure it no longer and went to my uncle's but was not satisfied, It seemed as though I wanted to see my mother and would go to bed at night and cry myself to sleep. My aunt treated me kindly and would pet me, but it was not mother and I was discontented.

My uncle soon proposed to send me to my grandparents in Madison county, Arkansas, where I was born. This was St. Paul, where my mother was buried. I sat on her tomb and wept. Grandma said she would be my ma, and was very kind to me. But readers, no one can take mother's place in the heart of her boy. I stayed with grandparents for four years, and then went back to Missouri where my brother lived.

Time had changed things and I was becoming a young man. I worked on a farm to earn my living. When nineteen years of age, carried away by hearing people tell buffalo stories and of great opportunities and wonderful adventures in the far west, I made up my mind to go there and seek my fortune as many other boys do even to this day. But, boys, when you get far away from mother and sweetheart, you will spend many loathsome hours out on the bald prairies where the howling coyotes never cease to send that lonesome, creepy, chilly feeling up your back. Your mind will go back home and mother and you will wish you were back enjoying the comforts of home. Boys, I have wasted nine years of the prime of my life roughing it upon the prairies.

When I was young and gay, dancing and sport-making was the pride of my life. I now bitterly see where I was wrong and I write these lines with a word of warning to the young not to follow in my path. May you be kept from temptation and not spend your lives as recklessly as I have spent mine. God's has come to me and said: "Orphan son, the rules taught you by your sainted mother, tell the world the truth of your past that others may take warning thereby. The courts of the law are directed by My word, and the Bible is the foundation of all law. Obey its teaching-- Thou shalt not steal; thou shalt not kill. The way of the transgressor is hard and all who disobey shall surely be punished. I sent the in spirit the father thou hast never seen; see His hand stretched out to thee, see it gently beckoning 'come.' And I hear my Father's voice in spirit saying, 'Come to my arms.'" God will forgive you and take care of all the things you have done in the past. Father, I will come and acknowledge to the world all of my misdeeds and I hope these few lines may keep others from temptation.

I went west in the spring of 1883 and I was twenty-one years old in March of the year. I was in Pueblo, Colo., in April and wrote back to my sweetheart. She cried when she received my letter and wrote me a long letter and when I read it I cried. She wanted me to come back. I wrote my brother and told him I would come back. He wrote me an answer to scare me and said if I came back I would be thrown in jail. He told me to stay away and he would settle things for me. I found out afterwards that this was a scheme planned by others to rob me of the property I had left behind. In May I went to work on a horse ranch at a salary of $40 a month, and a ranch man bought me a saddle and a blanket for bedding. I saddled a horse on the ranch and was directed to ride across the prairies searching for horses with a certain brand. The brand was the only mark which denoted who the horses belonged to as they were let run on the range. As I rode along I saw with surprised before me herds of deer, antelope, wolves and many forest lions. The sight of these animals made my hair stand on end.

I worked there about three weeks, and the boss was pleased with my action and nerve. A new horse was roped one morning whose color was blue, so they called him "Blue Dog." It took three of us to strap my saddle on him. I sprang into the saddle and dug my spurs into his sides and away he went, rainbowing to the west, over the smooth prairies. After going about eight miles Blue Dog and I separated. When I came to I saw a carriage coming across the prairie. I walked toward the carriage,beckoning for it to stop. I found it was my boss going to Wetumka for supplies. He asked me where Blue Dog was. I was vexed. "Damn Blue Dog," I said and burst out crying and told him I was going home.

"No," he said, and told me to get in the carriage, and go to town he tried to persuade me to go back to work , but I steadfastly refused. He then told me he would not pay me for what I had done unless I went back and caught Blue Dog. I told him I didn't want Blue Dog and that I had money of my own. So I caught the train and went to Colorado Springs, and from there to Denver.

From Denver I went to Cheyenne, Wyoming, and there got a job to drive a freight wagon which had ten mules hooked to it. This outfit belonged to the government cavalry at Castle Rock, Utah. We were ordered to go a distance of three hundred miles to Fort Arnold where the supplies were to be delivered. The Indians were very bad and the soldiers had several skirmishes with them. You may think it was fun, but I felt very different. In six weeks I returned and received a check for $108.00 for my pay.

I could have gone right back over the same route, but I did not like the work, so I took a train for Rock Springs, Idaho. I went to work in the coal mines at $3.65 per day. There was three hundred and forty white people and eight hundred Chinamen in camp. After working thirteen days a Chinaman call me a vile name and I landed him with a lump of coal. Down came the Chinaman and up came the Chinaman war flag. I was hidden by my white employers until night, and blacked up in disguise and took the train for Denver, thereby escaping murder by the Chinese.

From there I went to Trinidad and stayed three months. I then went to work on a cow ranch and stayed until the spring of 1884. I here met a Mexican who was working on the same ranch. He taught me the Mexican language. He told me he had a big horse ranch in old Mexico and was going down there to round up a bunch of horses and drive them to Texas to sell to cattlemen. He offered me $150.00 a month to go with him. I went thinking he was telling the truth. When we got into old Mexico he took me to several places and showed me several large bunches of horses, and said he and two other men would take me in partnership if I would help them steal them. And they would divide the money equally between us four. I said, "No." We then rode to a neighbor's house and after supper I stepped out and saddled my horse and rode about 20 twenty miles and laid down and went to sleep and when daylight came I went to a nearby ranch. While I was eating breakfast the Mexican came up with another Mexican with him. They told me if I revealed their secret we had talked about they would kill me. I made them a promise and I have kept it as I have kept God's word. I stayed at the ranch three days, resaddled my horse and rode over into Texas. I found friends there and went to work. I was scared for several months for fear of those Mexican, though I have never seen then since.

Chapter II

ROBBING THE SANTA FE EXPRESS.

I next got a job as a cowboy and with other cowboys helped drive a herd of cattle to Oklahoma in the Fall of 1884, located near Cottonwood Creek, eighteen miles from where Oklahoma City is now located. I went to Caldwell, Kansas, in the Spring and went to back to ranch work at El Reno Oklahoma, at the Flying V Ranch owned by a man named Tarry. The boss was named Coffey. We started in May on a round-up. The weather was wet, the grass short, and the horses were poor and slow. While waiting for the grass to grow and the horses to get flesh we were resting on the Cimarron River. One day in company with a man named Tom Colley, while playing cards and telling funny stories, he made a remark and said, "Boys, I believe the Santa Fe has got more money than Tarry." There was quite a lot of talk among the boys about money matters just then. Coffey and Colley would go off by themselves and set down and a man named Bill Bell counseled them. Three days later there were thirteen of us boys chose to go out on a round-up and sufficient lunch was prepared by the cook to last us two days. We rode northwestward for two days and came to a sandy ravine where there was three lone cottonwood trees and a pool of water. The orders from Coffey were to unsaddle our horses and to hobble them out, and on the morning of the forth day about sunrise, Coffey said: "Boys, are you hungry?" and then said: "Boys, I and Tom will go and get something to eat, and you will stay here, as we will not be long." They saddled their horses and rode to the northwest. That was an awful day to me. They came back late in the evening with some crackers and some canned goods.

Then the orders were given by Coffey to saddle our horses and ride. We started northwestward. Nothing had been talked of since we had been away from the wagon about the train robbery. We rode until about nine o'clock that night. The moon was shinning brightly. At last Coffey said, "Let's rest awhile, boy." Colley took from his saddle a sack that contained a bundle of cartridges and said, "Boys, line up here," and Coffey stood before the crowd and told them of the thing they were going to try to do. Colley was asked by Coffey if Bell would obey orders. Bell then was chosen by Colley to use a man that would put a penalty of death on the first disobedience of orders, or if either of us should reveal the secret of the orders, and Bell said he did not know of any one unless it was himself, so Coffey swore him in and Colley gave each one ammunition and Coffey assigned each one his duty that night. Bell held a six-shooter on each one of us as Coffey gave the orders of duty that each would perform that night in the train robbery.

My duty was to stand on the rear platform of the last coach and kick, shout and yell while the robbery was going on. We then got on our horses and rode to a water tank on the railroad where the express train would stop for water. The train soon came in sight and stopped at the tank. Guns were placed at the heads of the engineer and fireman and they were made to come down. I climbed upon the back platform and did as I was told. The other boys took the engineer and fireman to the express car and the expressman was compelled to give up the keys to the safe which in those days he carried. Only the safe was robbed and the passengers were unmolested. It did not take them but a few minutes and after they were through Coffey came back where I was standing on the platform yelling and shooting at intervals. He said, "Mister, you are alright," and patted me on the shoulder. He cried, "Let's go!" We got on our horses and rode all night, all day and a half of the second night.

After sunrise Coffey awoke me and said, "Let's ride." Looking around, all the boys had gone but six of us. We rode until dark, and was, and I was hungry, sleepy and tired! We then laid down and slept until morning. We rode all that day and until three o'clock in the afternoon before we came to the chuck wagon. I will never forget how good that meal tasted. By the next morning all the boys had gathered in and then we started after the cattle.

I had not yet realized what a crime I had committed, and did not until $6,480 was given me as my share in the robbery. I had never seen so much money before and I shook like I had a chill when it was given to me. I then began to get scared at what I had done, but worked on until September.

I then came to the conclusion to quit work and went to gambling, drinking and living a fast life. I tried to have a good time all through the winter of 1885, but I was haunted by fears, and when strangers would ask me my name, where I was from and my occupation, those simple questions would fill me with terror and make the cold chills run up my back, for my guilty conscience kept me in constant terror. I then made up my mind that I had better go to a small town and settle down, that I might overcome these fears. Therefore, I went to Corbin, Kansas, and started up in the livery business.

I was getting along nicely, had married, was happy and contented and had plenty of friends who knew nothing of the crime I had committed. One day in July a man rode into the barn and told me to take care of his horse. He said he was on his way to Wichita to see if he could not do something for Tom Colley who had been arrested and told me Colley said if he could not get out on bond he was going to turn state's evidence. Later I got a letter that said that bond would not be granted him and I had better prepare to get out of the way, So it was either leave home or go to jail and be brought to account for my past life, so I fixed things up to the best way I could and there was nothing for me to but leave my sweet, loving wife to weep and mourn. About three months elapsed and I took chances and went back and carried her away with me to another state.

Time passed slowly until 1888, when a messenger appeared and gave me a limited time to join a band which was not thoroughly organized. Some of the boys had been killed and another band had got short on help and they had to have me join them in another hold-up. I hesitated for several days and another messenger came and I was given a choice of either going to prison or joining them. So I rejoined the reckless band hoping I might soon get out of their power. But for nine long years I served with the devil and battled against man. I had that breaking feeling that I could never make more peace with them. I was a regular dare-devil and during those nine years I was wounded twenty-seven times, the last wound going through my bowels and bladder and making the physicians say I was unkillable by man. But I know trust in God and remember my mother's teachings and recall in horror my own terrible feelings when doing crimes against the laws of God and man-feeling of guilt so terrible that I hope none of my readers may ever experience it,

Chapter III

ON THE SCOUT

In 1888 1 started on the scout. I had had no experience in this life; want was staring me in the face. In July a man made friends with me and I met a brother named Butler in South McAlester and started to make a trip and had a fight. I got shot and this gave me a scare. Butler carried me to an Indian woman and went away, though the man who had made friends with me had gone to a house to get some lunch and got lost. In about three weeks Butler returned with the same man and he told a ghost story in reference to where he had been. I told Butler I believed the man was a spotter. He said he might be and we started riding in a few days and got in a big cluster of trees to rest our horses. We told him we were going to kill him as we thought him to be a detective and he must tell the truth, and if he did so, we would let him go. He admitted that he was a detective and showed his papers and this is the first time I was ever cruel to a man. We whipped him until he was bleeding and turned him loose. In the Fall I got a little money out of a small town in Texas and that lasted until the next Spring.

On May 18, 1889, I and Butler and Scott, Ike Rogers and Bob Powers went to a small lace in Colorado and found a water haul, and went to Canyon Gap and robbed stage on our way south to get a little expense money and made a jump to California and got a nice roll paid us all. I then went "into the earth" and thought I would quit this time. From there I went to Bloomfield Indiana, and when I got there I was a proud boy until so many strangers began to ask me so many questions. So it was the same old story, so I got scared again and went to Tennessee for the winter, but everywhere I went it seemed I could not rest. So in the Spring I went to Dallas, Texas. In June, 1890, Butler, Rogers and I went north to Michigan and we did not do any robbery that year.

In April, 1891, six of us went to Old Mexico to rob a bank on the border of Texas. The robbery had been planned in advance. The president of our gang had arranged with the cashier to have the currency divided into packages, and was to retain an equal share for himself. The robbery occurred on the 19th of June. We only got $36,000, while the bank claimed that they were robbed of $86,000. The cashier was greedy and had hid $50,000 for himself. He soon left that town and the last I heard of him he was living in Boston.

Chapter IV

TEXAS JACK

The name of Texas Jack was affixed to me in 1891. On June 28, when we thought we were out of danger on the prairies, we started to riding in the daylight. About nine o'clock in the morning we first spied trailing us a posse of Texas Rangers. The posse consisted of seventeen men riding toward us. I first thought it was a squad of soldiers going on a removal trip. Taking my field glass, I went out to one side and took a look to see who they were. I counted them at a distance of three miles away and we rode back to the trail and started off and we were beckoned to stop. Then we raised an answer "NO" and they made a charge, though we would not run, but got down and fought.

The fight started in the saddle and lasted about five hours before they would fall back. I got two slight wounds on my left leg and one man was killed and we lost some horses in the fight. We bound our dead man on the pack horse and carried him a distance of thirty miles to a sand bar on a creek and buffed him. It was about fifteen miles to a cow ranch and the rangers thought we were going to that point. They did not find us there. We rode that night until about midnight and lay down.

We had not more than got to sleep until the watchman awakened us for we could hear the noise of their horses feet coming down the trail. We mounted our horses and turned northward to another trail, thinking that we might give them the slip. About daylight rode into a cluster of bushes on a small creek. We soon heard the noise of a hound baying and we had to stand another fight. We killed the old trail hound on the first round and stayed in our little bunch of trees to rest our horses and then opened up fire on them about two o'clock in the afternoon and killed five head of horses for them and then rode about eight miles when the rangers made a charge on us and we ran into a ravine where we could hold them at bay and stayed there until night. The rangers stayed a distance of a mile away. This being the second day we were hungry, the horses tired and two of us wounded. We made up our minds to try and give the rangers the slip. We doubled back on our journey southwestward and came to a cow ranch about nine o'clock in the morning and hired a man to go to a supply store to get cartridges as we were running short. We got something to eat, rested our horses and hired a man to go on the ridge and watch so we could sleep. About four o'clock we were awakened by the approach of a man on horseback.

We thought the rangers were coming. We rode to meet our man who had gone after cartridges and met him coming about five miles distant. He told us the rangers were headed for the store. We rode to a high point and could see that they had changed their course. They had divided into bunches. They tried to surround us in a canyon, but we rode right into the nearest bunch and set them to going like wild geese. They lost three head of horses and we lost two, got one man wounded so bad that he died in five hours. We carried him that night, and buried him the third day in the morning.

There were but four of us left. We had but three horses and one of them was wounded. We were at a standstill. The rangers had us surrounded in a circle on a little creek with some timber and kept firing now and then all day long. About four o'clock they raised a flag of council. One man came down where we were and talked about our surrender. We told him that we would not and asked him if he was the captain. He said, "No." I told him to go back and tell the captain to come down. The captain came back with this man and they were on horses. I invited them down for council but we did not come to any agreement. I took the captain off by himself and asked him as a man of principle if he would rather see those men leave orphan children behind or open the road that we might ride on. He called to his man and gave orders to bunch the crew.

He walked upon the ridge a distance of two hundred yards where the rangers could see him. He waved his hat, circling to the right and dropped it behind him. He then raised it and waved it to the left and dropped it behind him. This was an order to line up. He then came back to where we were in the entrenchment. We then bound both down and tied them, got on their horses, rode down the creek and out of sight as the sun was sinking in the west.

We rode hard all night. When daylight came we had crossed over the Texas line into the Indian country, hungry, tired and sore from wounds and loss of our boys who had been with us. We went to a friend on the South Canadian, located on Walnut Creek, named George Shaw, where we had some fresh horses in pasture. We stayed about five days resting and then went up into the Shawnee nation and got out of hearing of those scoundrels.

In August, about the 18th, a man by the name of Rogers and I started to ride over into Kansas to meet Doolin and the Daltons. We met a full army of two hundred and twenty-eight Oklahoma tenderfeet looking for Texas Jack. After talking to us for a little while they said they were looking for this man and his crew and handed me a Dallas Daily News. I glanced at it and told them that I was in search of the same party, that I was a United States Marshal out of Purcell, Indian Territory, and that this man Rogers was from Kansas and was searching for the Daltons and Bill Doolin. A few words were passed and then they started on.

It was about ten o'clock Monday morning. We rode on about five miles, stopped and ordered dinner at a farm house. While waiting, 'Roger read the Texas fight in full to me and they said they hew not who to call him or who he was—that it must be old Texas Jack come to life once more. We both felt sad about the past events. After dinner we started on our journey, talking it over, we laughed about it.

While riding across a ridge from Deep Fork over to Cottonwood we accidentally looked behind us and saw a body of men riding in a lope toward us. They were heavily armed with pistols and shotguns. We let them ride up in a close range to within about a quarter of a mile, when we started to jog on a little faster and then they called for us to stop. Rogers was a little bit nervous and wanted to ride faster. The first thing we knew we found ourselves between two bunches of men. We crawled off into a ditch and the Oklahoma boomers killed our horses and Rogers wanted to give up. I told him I would not and if he raised up I would kill him.

We lay there until dark, in this ditch, and the Oklahoma boomers sat on the ridge and still surrounded us like buzzards. When darkness came I crawled up the trail with Rogers behind me in the ditch. I got to an old pap and told him to bring me two horses or I would kill him. He brought the two nearest ones and we crawled onto them and right then we started down the road. Rogers rode one that did not have a saddle and she was not fat either. To me it looked like he was riding a rail. We rode, turned the crow bates (sic) loose and tied a note in the mane of one of them reading like this: "You tenderfeet, plow corn, milk cows and don't hunt for outlaws and you will have more on Christmas day. If not, you had better be a distance away." It was signed "Bandits."

Then we got into a wagon and went to Kansas and found a man by the name of Smith and seven of us boys started for Waco, Texas, and stayed in the south during the winter of 1891.

In January, 1892, I went to San Antonio, Texas, to meet Brown and Smith and stayed around there until May and got a man who knew the lay of the country and his name was Watts and made a stage stand holdup as we were very nearly all in. We got about eight hundred dollars. We had some little expense money then for a small crew and started for California.

There was then six in the band. The band was controlled by an old head by the name of Dan Cummins from Buffalo, New York.

We robbed his own uncle of gold nuggets, more than we could carry at one time. It was in thifty-five pound bullions, and four nugget-bullions was a load for a Mexican jack.

We had a long trip through the glades for the Sand Voy (sic) Hills, dry and hot, and nearly perished for water; after getting those bullions it was awful hard to dispose of them. I said I did not want any more like that in mine for we were all summer making the trip. We did not get back to God's country. The jacks traveled slow and it was a hard job to get away with the bullion. In the Sioux nation, this side of Pike's Peak, Cummins went out to get some things to eat at a wayside store. He never did come back. Watts and I got cut from the bunch one night in a fight with the Indian soldiers and it was luck for us to get out. I met Gordon the next day with the trail of jacks and we changed the bullions of gold into Indian horses and went to the railroad where Rogers went ahead and chartered a car for Salt Lake

In the year 1892, we came back to Indian Territory or Oklahoma, and I came to the conclusion that I would quit once more and I tried to work, but I could not. Day by day strange questions would be asked, There had been a new gang sprung up, known as the Starr gang.

The name of Texas Jack had quieted down but in counselling with the president of the band he told me he would not let me off until the next spring as Henry Starr, Frank Chaney and Kid Wilson were men that could be trusted, as they had robbed Blue Jacket, Caneyville, Kansas, and the money divided five ways; the next on foot was Bentonville, Arkansas, and that he wanted me to go with them as it would take seven. I refused and would not go with them and the Bentomille Bank was robbed by seven men and the money was divided nine ways and each share was $1800, and then Starr went to Colorado Springs to wait and rest for time for orders of another plot. A man who was there on the sick list gave him away and it stopped his career by his being captured there.

I bought a farm in Arkansas and I thought I would be a farmer instead of a robber. The president told me again that I could not do this for he had spent so much money getting a route fixed for the year of 1894 that I had to go and help, as there was only a few men who had experience and there was a lot of new ones had gone to work around home, such as Cherokee Bill, (Bill) Cook, (Jim) French and others, like whiskey peddlers and hog thieves.

Chapter V

THE FIGHT ON THE "J O" RANCH

It takes money to live in a criminal life and lots of it. I have given $50 many a time to eat and sleep six hours and have a man guard me while I slept and rested. I would not ask him what he charged, but handed a "hand" to him when I got ready to leave. This was the reason why my friends would not give me away like others would. Some robbers would show their money and brag how easy it was to get—I never could do this it was always a hard job for me.

In the spring of 1894, in May, I set out to try another summer after a hard fight and argument with the president; he said he would be true to me until death, but admitted to some treacherous plans he had laid for other boys which would be the cause of getting them caught by marshals, He said they were no good, better out of the way and that he would die by my side. His sister, Sally, was inclined to me. Sally Dyer was good looking and was numbered one amongst the band, and I and the widow laid out a life line for the future to get married in the winter of 1894 and go to Old Mexico.

I had a hard summer. Seven fights with the marshals and got wounded four different times. One of these took place at the JO Ranch in the Choctaw Nation on the 12th of July, 1894 I lost my horse and Dyer was by my side in the beginning of the fight, but ran off and left me alone. They killed my horse, left me afoot and shot me under the jaw. There were six or eight marshals after me.

I kept my senses and showed that I could shoot as well as they. I killed three of their horses after the fight began. My horse was running, in about a mile he fell dead in the high grass. It was four o'clock in the evening I crawled through the grass like a snake and got outside the circle in which they were supposed to have me surrounded and went to the ranch.

It was now dark. I had three good horses in pasture there, but the marshals had taken them in their possession, so I could not get one that night. I waited until the next day upon top of a big hill between two rocks, just could crawl between them and hide. This took place on Monday. Tuesday, all day, I lay with a painful jaw without water. At night I went down to the brook close to the ranch and mixed up some mud and bound to the wound; this eased the pain.

On Wednesday morning I went back to my lone
rocks, where I could crawl in between, hidden until darkness came on. Thursday I was getting very hungry, the marshals were still gathering instead of breaking up. This was one of Dyer's plans to have me captured for the reward that was offered for me.

On Friday night I started to walk and walked until daylight, I came upon a small hut on the bank of Sand Creek. I had come about eight miles that night. I called, as they were not up yet at sunrise and an old lady came to the door barefooted and asked me who I was. I asked her if there was any of the men folks about. She replied, "l am Widow Harris." I asked if she would
cook me some breakfast. She invited me in and asked, "Are you the man that the marshals were shooting at the other day over at the ranch?" We formed a friendship, talked and ate breakfast, and I drank plenty of good sweet milk which she had. She dressed my wound and invited me to stay as long as I liked. I gave her a twenty-dollar bill and told her to have some biscuits baked about dark, as there might come along another hungry man, and bade her good morning and walked off up the road.

I did not go far. I lay down and rested all day.
milking time came I appeared at the milking gap asking the news of the day. She handed me a cup of warm milk, I drank it. As everything was quiet we walked down to the house and ate supper as she had prepared it and it was ready. She redressed my wound.

The next morning was Sunday and I was feeling brighter. The sun had risen and a scout was approaching while I was waiting for breakfast. He called at the old lady's house and asked if any stranger had been there. Just then I pulled the door from the old lady's hand and told him I was the man he was looking for. He was so scared he almost fell upon the ground; I invited him in to breakfast.

After we had eaten, I asked him who the horse belonged to that he was riding; he said it belonged to the livery stable at South McAlester. I told him that I would ride the horse and send it in to the owner inside of ten days, which I did. He told me there were a hundred men or more watching the neighborhood for me.

The next I was heard of was in the Creek Nation. I was riding along, accompanied by Tom Root, bound for Tulsa, when about eight miles from Tulsa all at once we were called to halt. We did not halt. We could not run, so we crawled off our horses and laid down in the old trail ditch. We lay about six hours until darkness came. They had killed our horses and we walked to the Verdigris Valley. We crept through the thick brush, winding our way down to Dyer's house, where we could get horses and saddles. I told Tom Root it was another plan of Dyer's to kill or capture me. I made up my mind to kill Dyer and sent him a note to meet me at a certain big log in the bottoms. I was there by myself when he came. He soon saw that there was something wrong and he began to cry and plead and beg. He pulled out a plot, explained it to me and read five letters that showed a start of a plan of a big consignment would be placed in an express car at Dallas, Texas, which would come over the M.K.&T. through the Indian Territory, and as I was in hard luck, I told Dyer I would help hold-up that consignment if he would lead the band. He said that was his intention and we reviewed the plot and talked about Tom Root's duty.

I could only answer for myself and for Root. I would have him in three days where he could see him personally. Root was held council with and agreed to carry out his part until death. Dyer then said, "Well, boys, everything is in readiness. In five days I will see you again." A letter was brought from Dallas, Texas, stating: "Boys, be ready; it will not be later than twelve days." This was signed "Thomas Hood," express messenger, Dallas, Texas. Then Root and I were taken by James Dyer over to Buzz Luck's house and here met a man named (Will) Smith. Then all five of us rode to the Blackstone switch and viewed the location and each one was stationed at a spot by Dyer, like performing a play.

"Twice before, inside the last three months," said Dyer, "I have placed men here in this position, and the third time must be a success. This express messenger has done his duty each time and this is our last chance as he will give the gang up, so he says, and now let's everyone keep closely hid and I will see that you boys, have plenty to eat every day."

After every breakfast we all played a rehearsal when the time came. The night set by the messenger, I had a warning come to me. When I arrived at Blackstone switch I told the boys unless Dyer came we had better not try to capture it alone. They all said, "He will be here before the train comes." I told them I would have to see it before I would believe it. Eleven o'clock came and Dyer had not showed up, but I had done my part up to that moment. The switch lock was cut and ready to throw and we had only fifteen minutes to wait. Tom Root said, "I will die right here." Smith and Lucky gobbled and a signal shot was fired, but no answer was heard. We all shook hands around and our positions were taken, all but Dyer's and it was vacant, and then the whistle sounded.

Chapter VI

THE BLACKSTONE TRAIN ROBBERY

Blackstone lies eight miles north of Muskogee, in the Creek Nation, on the north side of the Arkansas River and on the south side of the Verdigris River. This is known as the swamp land and there was a switch placed there for the purpose of unloading cattle and also a water tank. Our plan was to rob the Katy Express at this place. Dyer was to go in the express car and break the boxes open in which the money was placed at Dallas, Texas, by the express messenger. My duty was to throw the switch which would let the train go on the side track. I was then to take dynamite and blow the side doors and the end doors on opposite sides. Will Smith's duty was to catch the fireman and engineer and bring them to me. He failed in his part. When the engineer saw the switch light changed from red to green he pulled the whistle cord for a signal of marshals on the danger, as there were seven marshals on the train. They heard the whistle and sprang to their duty, which they were sworn to do by the express company, to safely guard this money through the Indian Territory, as this was known as the robbers' roost.

As the train stopped the marshals looked out and saw the moving form of a man running toward the engine cab. It was Smith trying to catch the fireman and engineer. Bud Ledbetter and Paten (sic) Tolbert were riding in the express car and began firing at Smith. Smith was running after the fireman. They both fell over a wire fence and never did come back. I went then to the engine and could not find anyone. The steam was rising high. I opened the fire-box door so that it might cool down instead of blowing up. Harkers was the engineer's name. He said he could see me when I pulled the fire door open. He felt somewhat relieved then and knew the boiler would not blow up.

I then went back to the express car, pleaded and begged them to come out as I did not want to harm anyone and that I had come for the express and I was going to have it, for it was not theirs. All this time they were constantly shooting at every object and at every sound, After pleading with them a short time and they would not surrender, I went to Tom Root and told him to stand pillar to post, as I could not find Smith, and he had let the engineer and fireman get away, so I would have to go on the inside and try and get Cudgel, the conductor. He said he would stay right there until I called him. I sprang upon the platform of the smoking car. I had my rifle and six-shooter in my hands. I opened the door and said, "Good evening, gentlemen."

There were three men in the car, I knew their faces as well as my brother's. Mr. Lionbaugh sat in the front seat, John McAlester sat about half way back, and Jim Stewart in the rear end. When I looked the crowd over, I could not help from smiling. I asked them all to lock their hands over their heads and rise to their feet, which they did. "Now, gentlemen, fold your arms, and sit down and do not move until you are asked to." I then pulled a two-bushel sack from behind my back and handed it to a young man who sat near. I asked him to carry this sack. He at first refused and said they would think he was one of the robbers. Mr. Lionbaugh told him to go ahead and obey orders. He then took the sack. I chose another man to search the left hand side and just then a man straightened up over on the right hand side and said, "I am a reporter for the Globe-Democrat," and smiled, and I said to him that he could search the right hand side for me then, so that he could know it all. He refused; I raised at him with my gun and he jumped straight up and fell on the floor with a harsh voice,

"And you will, won't you?"

"Oh, yes, you will," he said, and went right to searching the right hand side. A laugh was heard at him. The sack was passed through the first car; only a few had anything worth taking. When we got to the rear end, I ordered them to open the door and stand there until I came. I ordered them out on the platform ahead of me and thanked the crowd for the donation.

As I pulled the door to, someone said, "He must be a Methodist preacher." Then we entered the second car. I spoke to them mannerly as before and took them under the same rule. The newspaper man spoke up and said he was a man of his word. I started the two men down the aisle, searching as before. Just then a man rose to his feet on the left hand side, holding his pocketbook in his hand saying, "This is all I have." While the man was feeling in his pockets, I stepped forward and took it from him saying, "You look like a laboring man. '

"Yes, I am a coal miner from McAlester," he said. A lady sat close by with two babies in her lap. I asked him if this was his wife. She replied, "I am." I handed the pocketbook to the woman and told her to use this money for herself and babes and not to let this man have one 10-cent piece to buy whiskey with.

This changed the grandmother's tune, as she was then upon her knees praying all hatred and scorn to the robbers, saying that they had come to kill and to leave paupers. Just then she sprang from her knees to her feet, crying aloud as she clasped me in her arms, "God bless the soul who takes pity on the poor."

This was the first time in my life that I was ever cruel to women, for I had to poke her in the ribs with my gun to make her turn me loose, and the drunken man said, "Mother, he is not harming us," and he placed her in her seat.

I glanced ahead as the searching was going on in the car. On the right hand side sat a young lady with golden hair, stripping her rings and diamonds from her ears, preparing to drop them in the sack. I spoke to the searchers and told them I was not after the poor nor what the ladies possessed. I just simply wanted a little collection from those who were able to divide or bear my expenses until the next assignment, as we were after the express, not to rob passengers, but was just wanting some expense money. When they got to the rear end of the car they waited until I came back and the young lady tapped me on my shoulder and says, "Can't I go along, for you are my kind of people?" I told her no, for I would soon be overtaken and then would be separated from her, and to go her way and I bade her good-bye at the rear door.

I then entered the third car with my three helpers, placing these people under the same rule as I did the others. The boys soon got through searching this car, as there was not very many in it. I found the Pullman conductor hid in the drawing room of his car, and took him into the fourth car with me, this being the sleeper.

The lights were turned down. I told the porter to light up, and he said, "No," and shut up his fist and started toward me like a prizefighter, I gave him a punch with my gun in the short ribs and he fell to the floor. The conductor called to him and said, "Joe, turn up the lights or we will all be killed."

I says, "Yes, I would not invite you into my house in the dark.

The buck negro turned the lights on and began to get his guest out of bed.

There was one man refused to get up and said he was very sick. I told him that some people called me "Doc," but I took him by the shirt collar and called for the money. He gave up a small amount and declared that was all he had. He was the only man I argued with that night. I dropped him from the second berth onto the floor. This made him sick sure enough. He threw up like a man had been taking Ipecac. The porter got one rib loose and came very near dying by not wanting to light his car. When he got better in the hospital the doctor asked him if he met the robbers again would he refuse to turn up the light for them.

"I will always leave it burning," was his reply.

We went to the rear door and it was locked. We had to turn around and go back through the car, and this man that I had pulled from the second berth was still on his knees throwing up. The newspaper man stopped and asked him a few questions. He said his name was Brigham Young. I tapped him on the shoulder and said to him, "Look here, you are lying to me."

He looked up at me. I said, "Your name isn't John Brigham Young, who has so many wives in Utah, for I knew him personally."

He said, "No, and no relation to him. I am the governor of Missouri." The newspaper reporter replied to him, "You ought to have someone hold your head while you vomit."

We walked on out, and I could not find Gudgel, the conductor in charge of the train. When we got on the ground the young man who had carried the sack through the cars begged not to go any further.

I let him go back.- We were on the left side of the train. I ordered the men to go forward to the express car. It was a bright moonlight night and walking down along the side of the cars, as we were in the shadows of the coaches, everything was quiet. I whooped Root gobbled and fired his guns several times and and heard no other sound. We reached the express car and the doors were standing open. I gave each man his orders. The conductor had walked upon the platform the porter standing on the steps and the other men on the ground. The conductor said, "I have no match," and I replied, "I came loaded with everything," and went to hand him a match. As I raised my hand to reach upward, my eyes caught a shadow which came from between the two cars, a six-shooter in the hands of a man drooping towards me. I was so close I thought the intention was to hit me in the head and I dodged and turned my face towards the car so as to stoop beneath the sill of the cars against the wheel; as it dropped toward me the pistol fired and the bullet struck my body in front of the upper part of the left hip, ranging downward, cutting the bladder and the lower bowels, coming out on the right hand side of the back part of the thigh. I fired back at him and he swore that he had got the damned scoundrel at last. I whooped and gobbled and I could hear Root shooting on the opposite side of the train. I kept on firing at the noise in the express car until things came quiet in there. My help had run off and left me.

I sounded the signal that we had so the boys would know that we were ready to go. It was a keen whistle, Root came over to where I was. I whispered and told him I had been shot, and for him to stay there until I got part of the way to the horses so they could not come out and capture me. I took the sack of money and started toward the horses. I stubbed my toe and fell down, rubbed my leg and gained action of strength. About half way to the horses I whistled. Root came and we went to the horses together.

When we got there Smith and Lucky were there, and had their horses untied. I asked them where they had been all the time. "Out here," said Smith. Tom told them that I was shot and, "Help him on his horse." I was helped on my horse. Smith insisted that he would carry the sack. It made me so mad I drew my pistol to kill him, but Tom Root begged me not to.

We started and rode about a quarter of a mile when nature came to my assistance and called for action on my bowels and bladder. I told the boys I would have to get down. They stopped and helped me down. When nature had pursued its course, the boiling blood came from both organs. This was the first time I knew where I was shot. I felt the burning sting, but did not know where the bullet went through until then. I told the boys that I was shot through the bowels and bladder and Lucky said, "No, it cannot be, as you would have died before this."

Tom Root struck a match and examined the ground. "It's nothing but blood," he said. They helped me on my horse again and we started to ride and only went about a half mile and I had to let my system drain again. Draining my system five times made me so weak I could ride no further. I told the boys I was compelled to lie down. We were only two and a half miles from Blackstone. They took my blankets, made me a bed under a cliff of rocks and I gave them a gold watch apiece and fifteen dollars in money each and they took the sack of money and made a pillow for me. I laid my head on it and told the boys to go to Dyer's house, tell him the news and come back the next night and bury me close by where I lay and put a board at my head and tell James Dyer to write to my brother the last place where I was seen and take care of my saddle horse as long as he lived. "So good-bye, boys."

Chapter VII

THE ESCAPE

This was the night of November 13, 1894. I remember well, it was Tuesday, and the boys came back Wednesday to bury me and I was yet alive. They called for "Jack," but 1 could not speak, so Nancy came down and raised the blanket from my face. I raised my fingers to show her that I was still alive and she called for water and Tom Root brought it from the river in his hat. This soothed and bathed my tongue until the swelling ceased. I got so by daylight that I could whisper and tell them what to do. Anyone who has been shot knows how the loss of blood requires water. They came back on Thursday night with a jug of buttermilk and Indian food that they called Saufaka (sic),

I was resting quietly and they stayed until daybreak and went away. I told them to bring me a syringe and castile soap to get action on my system and a little turpentine to annul the pain. They came back Friday night and worked with me all night. I was not resting very easy and the boys undertook to stay by my side. One was watching the road, the other the horses. Root and Nancy were working with me when about one o'clock Smith came in and said he had seen five different bunches of marshals. I told them they had better go to the horses as I would try and get along and they bade me good-bye.

This was on Saturday. I lay there by myself and could look across the river to where the public road ran. I counted fifty-six in number. Just as they were out of sight I heard some one say: "Halt! Stop, or we will kill you," and I heard a volley, constant shooting and yelling, and it sounded to me to be a mile distant. I did not see the boys any more until after I went to jail. I lay there all Saturday night, all day Sunday, and in the evening about sundown a stranger walked upon me and asked me several questions. I told him that my father and I were hunting and trapping and that I was chilling and that father would be in after a while. He offered to wait on me and do anything I would want him to do and told me his sweetheart lived over in the house we could see through the bushes, about a quarter of a mile. As the sun was sinking, he started away.

I pulled my boots on, picked up my gun as a crutch and took the sack that had the money and watches in it and went crawling through the brush. During the night I wandered about two miles. I came to a fence and built a fire and laid down and went to sleep as the chickens were crowing for day. The very next thing I knew I heard a voice say, "Whoa, Sam." I raised my head to see where I was. Just over the fence a negro was catching his mule. I crawled up to the back of the fence and I recognized him. I asked him for breakfast. He helped me to the house. Coffee and cornbread was all I could eat. I asked him if I could lie down in the house and rest. His eyes bugged out like snowballs and he said: "No, Jack, for the marshals were here yesterday searching for you. You go away and I won't tell anyone you were here."

This was Monday morning. I walked down the road about three hundred yards to a briary flat. I lay down and dropped off to sleep. About the middle of the day I was awakened by a pounding sound. I discovered that a body of men was breaking down the doors of the negro's house. They rallied for about an hour and came riding by where I was hiding. The crew was led by the young man who had talked to me the evening before. They had my blankets and slicker tied on behind two of their saddles, a frying pan and tin bucket, I knew that they were mine.

I kept hid until about five o'clock in the evening. I raised up and fixed my clothes to go down and cross the river before dark. Six men were within twenty steps of me, riding right towards me, when I said, "Good evening, gentlemen." They came to a stop, inquiring how to get to the Vann Lake.

"You are on the right path," I replied. "Keep straight ahead."

Then they asked me what I was doing there. "Killing squirrels," I replied.

They asked me if I had any luck. I told them that I had only found three, as the wind was very high. They asked me to let them see them, and I pointed to my sack that was lying against the root of a tree. The sack had blood on it. I raised my gun to my waist from the tree and asked them if there was anything else they wanted to know. They said no, and rode on.

When about a hundred yards away I heard someone say, "That's him, I know."

I heard another voice: "I don't want him, do you?" and they started off on a trot.

I then took my sack down to the ford of the river and buried it under the end of a big log and waded the river and went to James Dyer's house, seven miles away by myself and stayed there until Friday evening, when the place was searched for me by three marshals and did not find me. I was placed on a horse and went to Mrs Reynolds' house. She put me in a cotton field on Friday night under a big log and cared for me Saturday, Sunday and Monday.

They burned the cane brakes in the Verdigris bottom to find me. On Tuesday they found my saddle burning and warned the neighbors close by if they did not turn me over to them they would burn their cotton fields and corn fields. This was the order of Judge Parker.

On Wednesday night Mrs. Reynolds sent a boy out to where I was and told me to get on the old mare and ride up to the house. She told me what orders had been given to the neighbors, and for me to go down the river about a mile and a half to a certain big log and the boy would meet me there and bring the mare back and give me a wagon sheet as it was raining that evening. I rode away and made my bed beneath a cottonwood log on the bank of the Verdigris River. It rained all day that Thursday and sleeted all night Friday night. I was wet and cold.

Saturday I was chilled all day. Sunday morning three little boys came to see if I was dead or drowned. The river had risen and the water touched the foot of my bed. The boys helped carry my bed higher on the bank. They then went back with the news about me. In about three hours James Dyer and his brother came with some dry clothes, built a fire and thawed me out, put me on a horse and carried me about four miles. They put me in a covered wagon with Smith and his wife and little baby. We started and drove through Wagoner, Okla,, that night and in eleven days we were in Seneca, Mo., where they cared for me until the 20th of December, 1894.

Smith was awful cruel to me. He was a drunkard and I told him one thing if he did not treat me and his wife better I would go to one of the neighbors and tell the story of the past. I was lying upstairs in secret and dared not call for a drink of water until after bedtime as it was a public place. Smith made friends with a man named Lawrence living close by and told him that I was sick with rheumatism and that I was a ranchman and that he would have to go back to the ranch and sell some stock to bear our expenses and he would not be gone over thirty days, and if he would take care of me he would be well paid for it.

Of course, Lawrence wanted to see me himself. He came upstairs and talked a little while and saw that I was in a helpless condition and my bed so filthy. At my request he agreed to take care of me. I was then taken and bathed with hot water and dry clothes put on me, and was wrapped up in a blanket and placed upon Lawrence's back like a papoose and he waded through the snowdrifts for a quarter of a mile to where he lived. There I was placed in a nice cozy, clean bed and Mrs. Lawrence was a mother to me. They cared for me the best they knew how. Smith went away and never did return.

God then came to me and promised me if I would believe in

Him, He would heal me once more. I did believe and am still trusting in His faith. Then the last week in February, 1895, I sent William Lawrence to James Dyer with a note for him to send me money, which was left in his care. When Lawrence got there and gave Dyer the note, he asked how I was getting along by this time. He told him that I was able to sit up and walk around on crutches a little. Dyer told him the mules I had asked for had been stolen and the wagon broke down and my three saddle horses were awful poor and the money that he owed me he had paid out on lawyers' fees on the other boys.

He said, "I will send him fifty dollars and tell him I will be there inside of fifteen days. You take care of him until I come and I will bring him money." He told Lawrence of my past life. Lawrence said it was something new to him. He came home on the fifth night of March and wouldn't talk that night, but the next morning sent his wife away from home and then sat down and told me what Dyer had told him about my past. He said he did not know what I should do. I told him that I would go away the next morning.

I went to my brother's home in Madison County, Arkansas, and wrote to Judge Parker that I was ready to surrender, let come what would. If he would send after me he would find me in the neighborhood of St. Paul, Arkansas.

On the night of March 17th, the marshals came after me. I went to Fort Smith with them on the 18th day of March, 1895. When the train arrived at the depot such a crowd of people I never had seen before was there. I could hear them from each side of the street: "That's him, in the open there."

Hundreds of people were eager to see a hero like me as I was taken from the cab to the jailer's office. When I was registered on the jailer's books, I asked if I could lay down as I was weak and of course the newspaper reporter was there. He had hunkered right down by my chair. Mr. Dobson was his name. He told me he wanted to help me out of my troubles and was a friend of mine. I told him that he never helped me into it, and didn't want his help to help me in deeper. He asked me for a short item.

"Your items won't buy me nothing," I replied, "and if it buys you anything I will pay you more money than the price you draw to keep it out."

He said that he would give me a short write-up anyhow and asked me my name. I told him that my name was Little Poor Boy, and my dad and ma were too poor to name me anything else.

The bystanders gave him the horse laugh and he got up and talked to the jailer a few moments and rushed out. I was then taken upstairs, into the hospital, to be treated and tormented to death by detectives, but my business was my own. When I went there I went to make this my home and did not intend to let anybody worry me every day. The detectives came around and asked me questions, told me tales of what they knew, but I would sit and smile and laugh at such foolish ideas man can draw about people they have never seen. There but one who knows about other people's business. and that is God alone.

Chapter VIII

CONFESSION BEFORE MEN

When God came to me and picked me up in the year 1895, He gave me strength to lisp the truth and tell all to men. As He still keeps me, I am trying to repay the wrongs in showing there is nothing in living without the spirit of God's redeeming power.

I went to jail on March 18, 1895, and told about a secret society to which I belonged, in which there were a large number of members; about the man who controlled the gang. He was a man who had been interested in the bandit work until he became great and had furnished outlines and would go as far in the work as to make towns and grounds, and get things right, and would get in with express messengers and get their friendship and get them to let him know twenty-four hours in advance by telegrams. He would have a certain number of boys rob their trains and he would share in the proceeds with them.

When I told the law these few words it made them more anxious, and they could not rest until I talked more. I did not hurry. "Take one's time" is a good motto. I wanted to tell the world how I got to be a robber and others wanted me to tell them so they could go and get the rest of the band for there were big rewards for the robbers. "We will give you a share," said an officer.

"I don't want money," I said.

"Well, then, what do you want?"

"I want to become a free man once more," I said.

"We don't know," they would say.

Time passed on, until the 15th of May. I was called to the private chambers of the court and was asked, "What kind of a promise would it take to get you to tell who is controlling the gang? Name it yourself. Can you tell us who the head man of these crimes is?"

"The man has taught me and many others. I know his name as James Dyer."

"Is he at the bottom of all these crimes? Can you establish that?"

"Yes."

"If this leads to a conviction of him, you will be made free; that is, if you will promise the Court of the United States that you will never commit or participate in another crime."

I promised him (Judge Parker) that I would never do so again and was taken back to jail and in three days came out and repeated my story, and it was written down. Names and places were taken where certain men and women would be found for witnesses to establish whether I had told the truth or not of certain crimes and depredations, and they found things just as I had said.

Time went slowly. News was brought in which greatly encouraged the court and everything was cheerful, until one day in July when the officers came in with James Dyer. Then a howl went up—it went through the newspapers, people became somewhat surprised, and wondered if it could be the truth that Texas Jack had told the court, or would it prove to be a lie.

On the 15th day of August, 1895, Judge Parker called court for the Blackstone train robbery. The jury was empaneled and the indictments were read to James Dyer, Buzz Lucky, Tom Root and myself. The jury was instructed that Texas Jack and Tom Root had acknowledged their part in the robbery, and that the confessions which they had made would be used to convict the other defendants. Then a motion for a recess was taken by the lawyers. It was granted until one o'clock.

Chapter IX

REED ON THE WITNESS STAND

I went to Blackstone to rob the train (I told them in my confession). There were to be five in it; the band was Dyer, Texas Jack, Tom Root, Buzz Lucky and Will Smith. We were to meet the train there on the night of November 13, 1894, at eleven o'clock. Dyer lived seven miles from that place and he said he would not leave home until dark, and if he did not come, it would be because of sickness that would keep him away.

He did not come and claimed he was sick. The train came. I was at my assigned duty just the same as I would if I went to the field to plow corn. I turned the switch and the train stopped. I took the dynamite with me and used it according to orders; I called Smith, who was to catch the engineer and the fireman. He failed and I could find no one but Tom Root who was at his duty. I told him to stay in his place and I would get help in the coaches. He wanted to leave and let it go. I next went in the smoker and found a car full of rough looking men; I found seven six-shooters, which I ordered thrown out the window. I told them I was after the conductor The reply came from the rear of the coach that he went out the door at the first of the shooting.

"What was the loud report?"

"Dynamite."

"How many charges did you touch off?"

"Four."

"Tell the jury what part of the train you used them at."

"I placed the first charge against the right hand side of the express door, which blew the door from its place, and it fell on the floor. The second one I placed against the end door and just then the door opened while the fuse was sparkling. Some of the guards kicked at it, and I had to hurry to get out of the way. It fell between the cars and went off and blew two ties in two. I crawled up on the steps once more and laid another down there and it opened the end door. I then heard loud cries, "We will not.' I stepped aside and waited and they all agreed to come out but Bud Ledbetter and Pat Tolbert. They said they would kill the first one who attempted to leave the car. I talked to them a while and they did not obey, so I laid another charge against the left hand side of the car door and it fell on the floor. That made four discharges and I could now see through the car. Had I wanted to kill the crew I could have done so by lighting a stick and throwing it in the car as they were in one end. They were shooting continually at me. The blaze of fire would go over my head most every time. I was standing in the gutter."

"What did you do then?"

"I went down to the engine."

"Did you find anyone or see anyone?"

"No, or I would have used them in going in after the express."

"Did you see the engineer lying behind this log?"

"No, or I would have taken him to the express car."

"What did you do then?"

"I went to the smoker and done my work and then visited the four coaches. I was not going to rob passengers had I found the conductor."

"How many passengers were there on board the train, or did you see all of them?"

"I went through four coaches and tried to see all of them. I did not find the conductor, though I saw most

"Who did you find in the last sleeper?"

"A man who said his name was Brigham Young. I said, 'You are not the father of so many children of Utah?'

'I was once governor of Missouri and interceded in getting Jesse James pardoned,' was his reply. I jerked him out of his berth onto the floor and then he dug up $14 in money, but he did not give it up. The Pullman porter was the only other person in the car, and he was a bulldog when he said he would not light his car and disturb the passengers. He doubled his fist up and said he was running that car. I made him think he owned it when I punched him under the left arm with

my gun and he turned the lights up at once, and the reporter of the newspaper said he went to the hospital. That was the only man who made a disturbance that night by disobeying orders."

"Then what did you do?"

"I had three men that I got out of the smoker go with me. One carried the sack and two did the searching."

"Did you know those men belonged to your gang?"

"No, they did not."

"Are you sure?"

"I am sure that they did not, and then I asked the Pullman conductor to go with me, and he went along down to the express car with his light.

" What did you want with a light?"

"Wanted one in the express car so we could see to sack the money."

"How did you know there was money in there?"

"I saw a telegram that was sent from Dallas, Texas, stating it would leave there."

"What would leave there?"

"A consignment."

"How much?"

"About $10,065; ten thousand and a small sum would be in the safe, and the rest in small bags, and that it would leave the 12th of November and on No. 2. We got a time card.

"Then what occurred?"

"I got shot right there, and if you had got a bullet through you it would kill you in ten minutes. I have some feelings yet, and the reason I know I was shot there is that blood came from me freely, and is still flowing from my bladder."

"Let's see if that is the fact," asked one juryman, and I showed them it right there. "And I got this far along without a doctor."
They now told me to stand aside. I was twenty minutes on the witness stand. This came to a test on August 15, 1895, and five witnesses were to show that I was telling the truth, and there were 106 witnesses rebelled against me. The president of the band was on trial, and he was three days, and the witnesses had come to protect him, and I was the guilty one. He had a
hard fight. For eight days the trial went on, then the jury went into the box with a verdict of guilty against Dyer in just eight minutes. He was held in jail until September. This was fixed with me, as the court had to get certain proper forms from a higher court than I was under, and it took time. I did not ask my relations to help me, as I did not feel that my people helped me into it, and God told me if I would trust in Him, time would bring relief to me, and I might be a free child of His. I am a free one, and God bless me

Chapter X

A LETTER FROM THE DYER JURY
Bellefonte, Ark., October 2, 1895.

To the Eighty Citizens and the Fort Smith Elevator:

Sam Jones says the dog that howls is the ne that is hit, It appears from the howling of the Elevator in behalf of the Wagoner citizens that they are badly hit.

Facts are stubborn things, and the more the Elevator distorts and mystifies in its labored effort to justify the eighty citizens in supporting Dyer's honesty, the plainer they show themselves to be in a large sized error. The Elevator 's labor has been long and terribly severe, but at last has been delivered of a small sized mouse, The Elevator lugs in Mr. James Cobb and all the good men of Wagoner who were brought to Fort Smith to testify for Dyer, and tries hard to confound James Cobb and others with the hog and cow skin thief.

It will only require a few words to explain to any unbiased mind that the good men, James Cobb and others, are not included in our letter, nor anyone else that did not testify. It would have been just as fair and showed just as good sense for the Elevator to have classed Grover Cleveland, Senators Jones and Berry among its good men as to have included Jones, Cobb and the When Col. smith asked the question of Jones and Cobb if they knew Dyer's standing among his neighbors, Jones answered that, Mr. Dyer was good for his contracts and he had traded with him for some time. His Honor, Judge Parker, stopped Jones, and told him Dyer was not on trial for his punctuality, but to answer yes or no, whether he knew Dyer's standing among his neighbors or not. Jones answered no. That is all gotten down, and Jones, Cobb and many others got down and never did testify for or against Dyer's character. Now, all fair minded men can see that the great labor

brought on the Elevator was brought on by a fool's conception. We are not surprised at the fool's conception of the Elevator from what we are told of its circulation. We are told while there it would-not require a hearty
man to walk outside of its circulation in an hour and a half. The Elevator is so full of the fool's conception that it dodges the issue and rushes to the defense of the good men.

Jones, Cobb and others that did not testify, but regard them as gentlemen because they did not testify falsely. They committed a huge blunder in trying to dictate to Judge Parker and made a grand mistake in convicting an honest man. We would suggest if eighty citizens can, without investigation, render a more honest decision than Judge Parker's court and jurors, after
investigation, that you men move down to Fort Smith and go into the decision business. It would be a vast saving to the government financially and if your decisions should all be in harmony with your idea of Jim Dyer, we are sure it would meet the full approbation of all classes of criminals in the Indian Territory. "But, Alas," says Burns, "the best laid plans of men and mice gang aft aglee."

The Elevator makes one broad assertion that is very flashy, for it is not supported by fact or precedent. It says that the people of Wagoner and vicinity are as law-abiding, honest and upright as any community in Arkansas or any other state. Take out your Starrs, Chaneys, Booths, Dyers, Reeds, Luckeys, Browns, Mitchells, Waitmans, Smiths, then skin deeper and your cattle and hog thieves and take a census of your population and there is no county or community in any state that will be reduced within loo per cent of what that county will be. If that assertion of the Elevator was true, there would be as many convictions of high crime in that court from Arkansas as from among those good people. The court records will show 98 per cent of all the convictions from the Indian Territory.

Such assertions as that of the Elevator as to crime in Arkansas being equal to the vicinity of Wagoner shows a diseased condition of the liver and bad digestion, and will if not taken in time, surely produce "night hoss."

The fact still stands in bold relief that Reed testified that Dyer secretly fed and moved Reed from his house and that fact is corroborated by Dyer himself, and it can't be rubbed out. Reed says that Dyer stole the lumber that built his house and hauled it of nights; that Dyer stole Edward's cattle, killed them on the Verdigris River, threw the hides in the river and sold the beef to the workman, and the hides were fished out to corroborate Reed; stole his lumber from one of the good signers of the affidavit. The two letters are now safe on file that Dyer threw into the express car directing Joe Dyer to go to Huntsville, Arkansas, and take a plle of the bank and look over all the good horses he could on the way. The bank officials were notified and moved their cash to Fayetteville.

Reed says Dyer sent a boy out to steal a mule to pay one of the workmen. All the house cost was the mules, There is a citizen now in Wagoner who received a part of the proof. There will be a gentleman at the next grand jury to swear One got his mare out of Dyer's stables and Dyer and brothers paid him $205 to stop arrest. Another man to swear he received a watch from Dyer that was identified by the owner as one of the watches that was taken in the Blackstone train robbery. Henry Starr says that Dyer wanted more than $900 of the Bentonville money. Starr says they rode sixty miles after the robbery and got to Dyer's house; he tells the same story as Reed about counting the money on Dyer's kitchen table, The post office inspector has now over twenty letters intercepted from Dyer, giving plans for various robberies.

We will close for the present and await your reply. We have an abundant supply of evidence that we introduce as rebuttal against you next. If this should throw you into a "night hoss" or jim-jams we will await your recovery with patience and good feeling for law and order.

THE DYER JURY.

Chapter XI

NATHANIEL REED'S REPLY

When a Times reporter called at the U.S. jail hospital, he found me a little worked up over the Elevator article written in defense of Jim Dyer and attacking me.

"That man knows he was in the Bentonville robbery by planning it," I said.

"He furnished the brains for the outfit that robbed the bank and shared in the proceeds. The band started out from Dyer's house to go to Bentonville and returned when they had done their work. I saw the boys and talked with them.

"I asked Kid Wilson privately where they were going, He said they would tell nobody unless they were implicated in it. I did not ask him any more then.

"When the gang left Jim's at night they were to go to Frank's twelve miles away and stop and let the horses rest, I saw Mrs. Frank Chaney at Wagoner at the show the next night. She told me to tell Jim's folks that the boys left all right.

"After the Pryor Creek robbery I saw ten gold watches at Jim's house, and he told me they were the ones from the Pryor Creek robbery and he wanted me to exchange one of them for him, but I refused.

"When the boys had ridden away to Bentonville, Jim told me he and Joe were to get $250 for the horse and saddle, from Jenny or Lengthy. After the Bentonville affair all came back to Dyer's. Jim told me: 'The boys all gave $75 apiece.' The boys themselves had received 1,800 apiece.

"When Frank Chaney was in South America he wrote regularly to Jim, who kept him posted on things here. I saw two letters from Chaney to Dyer myself.

"The moustache and wigs for the Bentonville robbery were

expressed from St. Louis to Jim Dyer. They came in a square paper box, with a sign saying that it was from a beard and wig factory at St. Louis. Jim was mad at this and so was Molly. Frank Chaney had sent them from St. Louis to Jim. After refusing to let the boys have the wigs, Jim one day turned them over to the boys. He told Molly he would not let the boys have them, and at last told Molly to let the boys have them as they paid money for them.

"Jim was always on the betraying. Henry Starr told me up here in the hospital one day, just before the Bentonville affair while the boys were collected around Dyer's ranch he and Frank Chaney went down in the Verdigris bottoms to try their guns and shoot some. Henry's gun was without a needle and both he and Frank thought that Jim Dyer had removed the needle. Henry had to buy another gun then, and he left the old one at Jim Dyer's. When I was in Oklahoma with Frank Chaney, he told me the same thing, that is—that Jim was suspected by them of letting the marshals know something.

"As for making love to his sister, Jim denies it very strongly. Why the Sunday before the Blackstone robbery she and another lady, who was stopping at his house, and myself, went out into the river land looking for some horses. We went back to Jim's; I then took Sally Dyer home and returned to Jim's that night to talk

"I had known Sally a long time before this. I first met her at the home of Jim's mother in the Choctaw Nation where I remained three months. Sally was then widow of three husbands. After the three months aquaintance, Sally and I were engaged to be married,

"James is also a small fox thief. He has stolen and pilfered many things from his neighbors. He killed many of his neighbors' cattle and threw the skins in the river after night. The hogs that he stole and killed couldn't be counted. He even stole his neighbors' corn and would sell it back to them in less than three months. To be a man, he could not. James Dyer has in. cited many to robbery. He sent a man to Bentonville to plot the town, and then did not think the plot was right,

and the boys came in and got a livery rig to see if it was right. Their intention was to rob both banks, but they changed their minds when they spied the inside of the town. The robbery money went eleven ways. The Caneyville robbery was done by three men, and that money went five ways, and the money was counted on Jim Dyer's kitchen table, and the Pryor Creek train

robbery was done by five men and one woman, and that money was divided eight ways, and Southwest City was robbed by Bill Doolin and four others, and that money was to go ten ways though it was not divided honestly, for I know it was not. Some in the band ran off with it and when it was spent would sneak back and tell 'ghost' stories. There are some sneak thieves, that is what makes things unbalanced.

"Speaking from my own experience, the last four years I rode the plains, 1 have ridden them most of that time by night. 1 could ride from Mexico to Illinois at night and never be seen while the sun shone. Many a time I went five days at a time without a bite to eat, and so cold I would be half frozen. I would ride by the farmer's house and smell things cooking, and might have

met death if I should have stopped and even asked for something to eat. I once was accused in Fayetteville of stealing a horse, but no one could prove it. As I always did not believe in stealing small things, and I knew it was not right, although I had taken horses from those I sometimes met when hard pressed, when my horse would be worn out and I would have to make my escape from being killed or get the first rope or go to the penitentiary, but I did not engage in petty horse stealing. I had a hard struggle with my fellow man, though now I trust to God for help. It seemed at times, that the saddest, darkest hour is just before day, I find that it has been the brightest one in life. God has promised to everyone who will obey his commandments, everyone, He has promised even the vilest sinner that comes to Him for repentance."

I was in jail twenty-three months, and was paroled out to go and see what kind of a life I could live. I trusted myself and men watched me wherever I went, and when times came, once every twelve months, I was ready to answer to my year's report. Then five years rolled around I was granted a parole of discharge, a free man.

Every time I returned to the city of Fort Smith, I met many friends reaching out and shaking hands and saying: "Once a robber but now a preacher." Understand, they invited me to their parlors with the view of assisting in teaching children right from wrong. I have been a free man from jail ever since the tenth night of September, 1896.

Trusting, kind readers, by reading of my past life that it may place a remembrance in your minds, that will keep you from evil things. The miserable life of all is when you can see the green grass and cannot stroll through it on your way home. I have roamed this wide world over, and as my mother taught me when I was Young that a rolling stone would gather no moss and an unbeliever never shall swing on the crown.

While up in jail, I found, besides men, at one time there were thirty-nine women who received their ration in tin pans for breakfast. This was our bill of fare: For breakfast, a tin cup of black coffee, half a loaf of bread, a slice of fat bacon, a small Portion of sorghum molasses.

"You can eat until You bust or set it aside and starve, just as you choose," this was the jailer's blessing. Now for dinner: a hunk of cornbread two inches thick and five inches square, a small portion of beef, one kind of a vegetable placed in a quart pan. This came twice a day. Do you want to live on it? If so, try it. The jailer was good to me, and all the guards also. The doctor came every morning, and all who were feeling bad would report to him saying: "Here I am." His request would be: "Let me see your tongue," and ask the number of your cell and he would pencil it down.

I have seen five lying dead upon the floors in jail at one time. I have seen thirty-six chained together, two by two, bound for the penitentiary, their sentences ranging from one year to ninety-nine. The women went just as well as men. It was a rule of the court to make a shipment every three months, which never failed. I have seen three hundred and eighty-six in jail at one time. The cook would find lots of trouble to feed this

gang. There were all nationalities; the deaf and dumb and blind— all for various crimes, and there were seven hanged, among them being Cherokee Bill and his pals.

CHEROKEE BILL'S LAST REQUEST
TO JAIL MATES BEFORE
GOING TO THE SCAFFOLD

Well, boys, try and shun the place where I am going, and John Pearce and George, two brothers, our last battle out to the gates, and I want you to keep in mind there is a judgment day to come for all. I know from a revelation which came to me last night. The doors were opened for me to gaze in the pits of hell; and I am praying for you all to reform before it is too late, and there is a hereafter. You people stand there musing and gazing on me. You think I have been quite a hero. I killed three men while I was on the scout, and one in jail while trying to get my freedom, but did not make my escape then. I want you to know it was God's will that I did not get the keys, and it was God's power that caused the spring of that six-shooter to break and it was my sister that brought me my gun in a jug of buttermilk.

A piece was sawed out of the jug and sticks braced in to keep it from shaking, and I hope that she will not be blamed, for she loves me as your own sister loves you.

Again, I beg of you to reform for there is a God beyond here, and I know if you ask and trust you will have a home over on the Other Shore, for God promised me a home if I would teach the rest of my life. I hope you will pray for me, is my last wish, and that my mother and sister will place a bouquet upon my grave each Decoration Day, as a memorial of trust in God. As I walk to the scaffold, I leave you all behind, for l have to die for the crime I did on this earth. I bid farewell to all of you. It won 't be long until God will call you all home.

Good-bye, I must die like a man.

Here ends the original text of the 1911 version

Appendix

Muskogee, Okla., January 28, 1936.

To Whom It May Concern :

This is to certify that Nathaniel Reed, known as Texas Jack, and myself were born and reared in Madison County, Arkansas, about eighteen miles apart, and ran together much when boys. When Reed and I became grown ups, I became an officer of the law and Reed joined a band of criminals.

The next time we met was in the Blackstone Train Robbery, November 13, 1894. When Reed was acting as the leader of the gang and I was acting in my official position as U.S. Deputy Marshal, and just happened to be on the train with a posse of men at the time of the hold-up, and the fight was on. The train was held up for one hour and 40 minutes. During this time Reed threw four sticks of dynamite, each one having its effect, blowing off train doors and perfecting entrance into the train.

During this battle I got my boyhood friend, Reed, through the body. His pals took him and got away with him. It was estimated that 500 shots were fired in this battle by the officers and bandits. Reed was the only one touched. They secured a handsome sum of money and other articles from the passengers only. Reed laid away for five months without medical attention. He notified the court that he was ready to give up, and was brought in to the government hospital in a critical condition; entered his view of the train robbery and gave valuable information which led to the breaking up of the bad band of outlaws. He was given a light penitentiary sentence which was suspended during the court for good behavior and he was released.

Forty-one years have passed and when Reed called on me at my home, I recognized him as the same person I had known in my childhood.

It is agreed now between Reed and I that there is, nor never has been any ill will existing between us, and I am proud to give him this letter.

(signed) J.F. LEDBETTER.

Note:

James Franklin "Bud" Ledbetter was a Deputy U.S. Marshall in the Indian Territory. He was born Dec 15, 1852 on his Grandfather, George Washington Ledbetter's farm at Aurora, Arkansas, seven miles south of Huntsville. Aurora was on the banks of the War Eagle River. When Bud was seven years old, his family established their family farm on Ledbetter Mountain near the old community of Mante, Madison Co, Arkansas. Bud was the son of James Franklin and Sabrina Tennessee Reeves Ledbetter. His father died in 1862 and after his mother died in 1870, eighteen year old Bud went to Indian Territory and worked as a railway guard for Wells Fargo for two years. In 1872, he went back to Madison Co, Arkansas to resume farming. Bud married Mary Josephine Terry June 28, 1874. In about 1876, Bud and his family moved to Coal Hill, Johnson Co, Ark. He was employed first as Town Marshal, but soon became a Deputy Sheriff. In 1894, Bud again moved his family to the Indian Territory and took a job with American Railway Express on the MKT train between Kansas and Checotah,IT. In Nov 1894, the infamous Cook Gang tried to rob the MKT "Katy Flyer" just north of Muskogee. Bud Ledbetter was the only guard on the train but he shot it out with the Cook Gang and forced them to retreat. His bravery and marksmanship caused him to become a local hero. The next year he became a Deputy U.S. Marshal in the Indian Territory working out of Judge Parker's Court in Ft. Smith. In 1897 Bud was in charge of a posse that was in a gun battle with the Al Jennings Gang and killed or captured them all. In 1906, Deputy Marshal Bud Ledbetter arrested Mack Alfred for the murder of Cicero Davis. This was a part of the Porum Range War that had been raging in Muskogee County from 1906 to 1912. After many years as a Deputy Marshall, Bud Ledbetter became the Sheriff of Muskogee County. He was an honest man and was respected by the citizens of Muskogee County. In 1928, he retired from law enforcement and lived on his farm in Muskogee County.

From the Muskogee Times Democrat

RETIRED OKLAHOMA PEACE OFFICER DIES
"Uncle Bud" Ledbetter, 84, Had Battling Record

July 10, 1937—Muskogee, OK—Funeral services will be held here Saturday afternoon for J. F. "Uncle Bud" Ledbetter, 84 years old, for a half century a battling Oklahoma and Arkansas peace officer, who died Thursday night.

He was born in Madison County, Arkansas December 15, 1852 and died July 9, 1937 in Muskogee, Oklahoma.

The services will be held in the Muskogee Civic Auditorium. Members of the United States Marshal's office and city and county officers will attend in a body.

"Uncle Bud," as thousands knew him, retired to a farm near here in 1928 after service since the 1890s as special officer, United States marshal, policeman and police chief in eastern Oklahoma. He began service as a peace office in the 1880s as an Arkansas deputy sheriff.

Saint Paul Mountain Air March 23, 1895

"Texas Jack" Captured
Supposed to have been a member of the Cook Gang
Officers Claim He is a Member of a Gang of Horse Thieves at
Wagnor, I. T. - Spaulding Orredyke, Alias "Darby," also
captured.

Nate Reed, alias "Texas Jack," accused of stealing horses and
supposed to be a member of the noted Cook gang, was captured
Saturday (3/18/1895) night at Andrew Cochran's two miles west
of St. Paul.

A posse of eleven deputy Marshall surrounded the house and
commanded Reed to come out and surrender or they would fire
the building. He complied with the request and the capture was
accomplished without a shot being fired.

Spaulding Orredyke, alias a friend and supposed accomplice,
was captured at the same time and place, and both were taken to
Ft Smith Sunday.

It is claimed by the officers that Reed had stolen horses near
Wagoner, I. T., and that he was captured once before and was
wounded while fleeing from the officers.

Reed was born in Missouri, but principally raised by an uncle
near here and has made several trips in and out of the country,
claiming that he had an interest in a horse and hog ranch at
Wagoner, I. T.

About a year ago he came here with a bunch of horses, traded
and sold them taking about fifty head of cattle away with him, but
has been looked upon with suspicion by a number of people here.

Reed came into St. Paul about two weeks ago by way of the
Frisco railroad claiming to have rheumatism and to sick to ride,
but it is reported the the marshals examined him and found the
wound that was inflicted at the time they claimed he escaped.

Reed is a relative of some of our best citizens here, who deny the
report about his being wounded, and believe the officers have got
the wrong man, and that he will be back in a short time.

He had no weapons at the time of the arrest.

Reformed Outlaw

Dies Peacefully

Tulsa, Okla. (AP) — Reformed outlaw Texas Jack, who rode with the Daltons, Bill Doolin and Henry Starr, died Saturday with his boots off.

Jack whose real name was Nathaniel Reed passed on peacefully in bed at his home, an old man of 87. No immediate relatives survive.

The crusty old timer still bore 14 bullet wounds, scarred mementos of his life as a desperado in Indian territory, now Oklahoma. He boasted of four train robberies, seven bank thefts, three stagecoach holdups and two gold bullion snatches.

His career of crime came to an it abrupt end before judge Isaac C. Parker at Fort Smith, the famous "Hanging Judge of Arkansas," who released Jack when he turned state's evidence. It resulted in conviction for his confederates.

The penitent badman then became an evangelist. He toured the country with a wagon and team of horses, preaching the moral or respectable living. Reed later appeared in wild west shows billed as 'Texas Jack, Train Robber'.

He was born in Arkansas in 1862 will be returned to his native state for burial, friends said.